EMOTIONAL

CHILD
ABUSE

This book full of commonsense, will help good parents become even better parents who will guide their children on the road toward greater emotional maturity

Using an illuminating blend of psychological advice and Scriptural teachings, the author shows how fathers and mothers can clear the hurdles put in their path by our neurotic and confused society.

His plea to parents not to delegate responsibility for their children's sexual and emotional education to teachers, social workers and psychologists should be heard and heeded by all.

— Conrad W. Baars, M.D.

JOHN   C.   TORMEY

EMOTIONAL
CHILD
ABUSE

ALBA ▲BOOKS

ACKNOWLEDGEMENTS

The Author acknowledges with grateful thanks permission to quote from their publications kindly granted by the respective Publishers for JONATHAN LIVINGSTON SEAGULL, THE PROPHET, WHY WAIT TILL MARRIAGE, LOVING AND CURING THE NEUROTIC.

Special gratitude is due to Tom Currier for his creative illustrations and to Jean Marie, Laurie, and Marilyn for their affirmation and encouragement.

Curt Baars, M.D., Thomas Flaherty, Ph.D. and Edward Sullivan, Ph.D. also deserve my gratitude for being special friends and sharing their expertise.

Much appreciation is due to Lloyd and Lynn Willey, the magnificent parents of Larisa whose winning smile is on the back cover.

Cover photo Paul R. Schell, Youngstown, Ohio

Library of Congress Catalog Card No. 78-73622

ISBN   0-8189-1158-1

© 1979 by Alba House Communications, Canfield Ohio 44406

Printed in the United States of America

DEDICATION

"The greatest good we can do for others is not to give them of our wealth but to show them their own."
— *Cardinal Suenens*

I'm proud to dedicate this book to my Mom and Dad who are so very much in love with each other that their affirming and affectionate love was always available for their three children.

The

Author

Since his ordination in Providence, R.I., in 1967, John Tormey has become widely known through his over 50 articles in Catholic publications and his books, ROCKS ARE FOR LIZARDS, PRIESTS ARE ONLY HUMAN, PIE IN THE SKY.

Father Tormey attended St. Bernard's Seminary, Rochester, N.Y., and studied Theology at Catholic University.

Presently, Chaplain, St. Xavier's Academy, Providence.

Department of Education   November 6, 1978

Rev. John Tormey
Our Lady of Fatima Hospital
St. Joseph's Unit
21 Peace Street
Providence, Rhode Island

Dear Father Tormey:

I have just finished reading your excellent book
Emotional Child Abuse. What follows are a few words
about the book.

This book serves to fill the void in this area. A
great deal has been written about physical child abuse but this
text is unique in that it gives parents an opportunity to examine
what they are doing which might contribute to the emotional
abuse of their children.

In this book John Tormey asks parents some very basic
questions:

Do you like who you are?
Are you satisfied with the person that your child is
imitating and emulating?
What priority is your parenthood in relation to time,
attention and energy?

The honesty with which parents answer these questions will
give them insight into their potential for the emotional abuse
of their children.

Emotional Child Abuse is a must-reading book for parents and
teachers. The writing is straight-forward and impressive.

Sincerely,

Edward A. Sullivan, Ph.D.
Associate Professor

Education Department

IN KINDNESS AND IN TRUTH

This book is a worthwhile attempt at fleshing out for parents some pivotal ideas in contemporary Catholic thought.

First is the Pro-life insight that reverence for life begins with the unborn - begins, but does not stop there. Parents are challenged to grow in reverence for their children through infancy, toddlerhood, school-age and adolescence - in short, " at every stage of development. " This reverence is shown by affirming the child through a positive, optimistic attention.

A second pivotal idea developed by this book is that parents are the image of God for their children. Concretely, this means that their parental attitude toward the children is to be a mirror of the Creator's attitude - one of affirmation and love.

The author applies these insights to a series of topics such as perfectionism, favoritism and sex-education in a few succinct paragraphs. A quotation follows, usually from Scripture, that illustrates the topic treated. The style is direct, challenging - one may almost say prophetic.

I recommend this book to Catholic parents. May it spur their ongoing conversion of heart and mind to authentic Christian parenthood.

+ Daniel P. Reilly
Bishop of Norwich

November 30, 1978

INTRODUCTION

It was a hot July afternoon so I decided to go to the beach. I found a vacant spot to lounge my body and settled down for a relaxing experience of sun and surf.

Within the hour a family from Georgia drove up, surveyed the beach and made the decision to crowd my few feet of land.

The father was an ugly little man with a Hitler mustache and sat like King Tott on his sunchair. He spent the afternoon ordering his family to his service with obscenities and degrading demands such as "hey, dummy, get me a beer".

If his children turn out to be Dixie dummies, then I know where it started. His mousy little personality made them feel inferior and insecure.

EMOTIONAL ABUSE

Unfortunately, this story has too many common variations. We hear of the bizarre tales of *physical* child abuse but far more common are the stories of *emotional* abuse: parents who infirm their children with a degrading feeling about their self-worth. The child feels sick—when he or she thinks about himself or herself.

This contagious "dis-ease" of the human personality is called an inferiority complex. Parents are largely responsible for passing on this crippling infirmity—that can paralyze a child with fear and insecurity for a lifetime.

Freud offers the concept of the id—ego—super-ego in his quest to understand human personality development. The child is born with the raw material of humanity—an "id". Hopefully, this person will become a secure, confident personality —an "ego" and say "I am".

The process is accomplished with the help of an emotionally healthy "super-ego"—parents who say "I already am". Unfortunately some super-ego parents are so messed up themselves that the child imitates and emulates a poor example in his quest to become an "ego."

Television excites our imagination with the stories of children being lost and raised by dogs and wolves. The child, of course, grows up acting like a wolf. Even Tarzan learned all the agility of his tree-swinging from the apes.

These stories are not just fiction. In California police found a girl with thirteen years of existence

4

living with a cat in the back room of her grand-parent's old cottage.

She walked on all fours, ate her food from a dish and cleaned herself as the cat had taught her by imitation. She had no human love, learning or language. She was still a mass of personhood without human personality because we receive our dimples from our genes but our personality from our family.

Let's return to one of your finest hours. You conceived a child who rested comfortably in the amniotic sac for nine months getting three square meals a day. The growing child got very satisfied with the warmth, comfort and nourishment of the womb.

Then one day the trauma arrived and the child experienced the scariest moment of its life—birth into the unknown. All of a sudden it was grabbed by a masked man who looked like the lone ranger. He turned it upside down and slapped its fanny—as it cried its lungs out. It was then passed for a washing to a nurse that looked perhaps like Tonto.

Later on a fellow with a big snozzola that looked like a shotgun bearing down on it was hitting the glass protection of the nursery saying: "kitchie koo, I think the baby has my nose".

Of course, "the kitchie kooing" the warm, loving kisses and embraces assured the child that everything was okay. It was loved. It was secure. When it cried, everyone turned and gave their attention.

STEPS IN DEVELOPMENT

How do children develop? There are different concepts. Perhaps Eric Erickson has one of the better theories when he relates development to going up a staircase. Each step has its own maturity with the next step building on the foundation of the one before it.

If one step is weak and incomplete then eventually all the succeeding steps will fall and crumble. *The building process will return to the weak step and attempt to start again.*

Parents are largely responsible for setting the foundation and then helping the child grow step by step until it can walk alone.

With this concept, no one attains full maturity and retains it forever. Every phase of life calls for affirmation and encouragement.

All people need someone else to affirm them because it is so difficult to break from the vicious cycle that keeps us inferior. We can try to assert ourselves but often that process only becomes a pursuit for pride and power.

Parents are the prime affirmers. If they fail, then their children will be left with the agony of assertion. They will groan for a lifetime trying to feel good about themselves and striving to prove it to others.

What is affirmation? Conrad W. Baars M.D. the famous Dutch-American psychiatrist has defined it to our best satisfaction in his book "Loving and curing the neurotic":

Affirmation presupposes confident expectation and

uninterrupted attention to everything that happens in the other, to all he is not able to express and to all the anticipated good that lies within.

The very opposite of affirmation is denial. We deny another by reminding him of what is not yet good in him, by thoughtless criticism, or the giving of premature advice without really listening.

When people are convinced of their self worth, they will not suffer the anxiety of criticism, or the burden of conceit which is a futile fight for recognition and approval.

Their confidence will set them free from fear and failure. Criticism will not discourage their dreams. They will start again when all seems lost. They will be free and detached from the constant need to be pampered. They will be comfortable being alone and not overwhelmed with loneliness.

Parents can make this happen by reminding their children of what is good in them and constantly encouraging them to fulfill their potential with realistic goals.

Then someday they'll enjoy the award of their greatest achievement: the day when their child will walk alone, secure and self-confident to pursue its own destiny: the day that they hoped for from birth, when they would set it free as a young sparrow from the nest to fly alone.

Of course, if parents have done their job right the child will always come back because it loves and respects them for their self-sacrifice, because it seeks the wisdom and encouragement of such fantastic parents.

Parents! Give yourself a treat and linger your mind on the beautiful words of Kahil Gibran:

7

"Your children are not your children
They come through you but not from you
And though they are with you
Yet they belong not to you
You may give them your love
You may house their bodies but not their souls
For their souls dwell in the house of tomorrow".

You gave birth to children to set them free—
not to keep them dumb, depressed and dependent.
As Kahil Gibran further writes:

"You are the bows from which your children
As living arrows are sent forth."

Steady the bow with your values and discipline.
Set the target with realistic goals. Gently release
the arrow from your grasp because once it has
taken flight, there is little you can do to determine
the direction.

Perhaps at this time you are ready to tell me
that you have steadied the bow and set a good
direction, but that your adolescent's friends have
lead him/her astray with their radical, permissive
ideas and their captivating influence.

You have a legitimate criticism. Yes, adolescent
children are quite impressionable. They are seeking
a new identity—to be John Jones and not Mr. and
Mrs. Jones' son. They crave recognition and the
thrill of adventure. They want to be a somebody
among their friends.

Of course if you have made them a "somebody"
with your affirmation, if you have encouraged
their self-identity with your recognition and developed their potential and hobbies with enthusiasm,

8

then you might not have to worry about their friends leading them astray.

But, if you are hurt and frustrated with their "know it all" sarcasm, then find consolation in the wisdom of Mark Twain. Perhaps your son will say it someday as well:

"When I was seventeen, I was ashamed of my father's ignorance but at twenty-one, I was surprised how much my father had learned in four years."

ACCEPT RESPONSIBILITY

In a recent discussion with parents, I introduced some of the ideas in this paperback. A few were upset that I put so much responsibility on them and argued that I place the blame on the children. I knew right then that they were the exact people I was trying to smoke out with my reflections.

A child cannot give what he does not have and parents are directly responsible for instilling values, beliefs and goals so that a child can grow up with a sense of responsibility—which transposed means the "ability to respond".

I still maintain that *parents hold the greater share of responsibility* for their child's development and behavior. Adolescent peers come second, environment places third and heredity a distant fourth.

You might not agree. That's fine but at least formulate your opinion and maybe for the first time in your parenthood take the opportunity to analyze your influence on your children.

Do you like who you are? Are you satisfied with the person that your child is imitating and emulating? What priority is your parenthood in relation to time, attention and energy?

Some years ago a good friend gave me a fine cigar that he had been saving for his child's birth. It looked terrific in the cellophane but when I unwrapped it, the cigar fell apart in my hands.

Some parents are somewhat similar. They look terrific in their leisure suits and foxy outfits but when they undress to their underwear in the privacy of their parenthood, they fall apart.

Read this book. Be honest with yourself. Are you satisfied with the affirming love that you are sharing with your children?

Of course, the best way to rear healthy and happy children is to work at a happy marriage. The greatest gift a father can give his daughter is to love her mother. Likewise the best gift a mother can give her son is to love his father. There is no doubt about it—happy marriages are given the better odds for happy children.

This book is particularly written for good parents who would enjoy a few quiet hours wondering if they are doing everything possible to rear emotionally healthy and happy children.

It is a chance to take inventory. Perhaps you have to stock up on *patience*. Or maybe this year it is *trust*. Your children need different commodities for various years of their growth.

Resource yourself. Do not allow your soul-storehouse to go bare with the qualities that your children need. Have plenty of love, loyalty and laughter on hand; more than enough patience, prudence and positive thinking and let affirmation, affection and attention be running over in abundance.

And remember, if you really love your children be prepared to suffer. Your birth pains will never cease. They will reoccur each time your child develops to a new stage of growth.

I have used a generous helping of scripture to headline the characterizations which follow because I think it is the finest psychology book on the market. I am convinced of St. Paul's advice to his friend Timothy: "All scripture is inspired of God and is useful for teaching the truth, rebuking error, correcting faults and giving instruction for right living" (Tim. 3,16).

May the short Scriptural introduction on each following page linger in your heart and become a prayer when you need it the most. Do not underestimate the power of God's word. It is still miracle working.

Now it is time to meet the cast who will role play the various possible causes of emotional child abuse and its infirming effects. I apologize that they illustrate many negative characteristics but often the positive is highlighted by being conscious of the negative.

PLAYING DEAD

Parents who act out fainting spells, nervous breakdowns, heart attacks, and other Oscar winning performances instill a guilt complex in their children: "Do not displease me. You'll be the cause of my emotional destruction or death."

When persuasion and reason fail they pull the ace and feint the ultimate pressure—the game of "roll over and play dead". They say in effect: "meet my demands or suffer an agonizing guilt the rest of your life."

Children who have experienced this horrible pressure never really get over it. They are afraid to make a personal decision that might offend because it always seems to be a life or death decision.

Fear and guilt are dirty tricks to play on sensitive children. They cannot defend against it and their dependence is assured unless they decide to suffer the agony of emotional withdrawal. Parents! Be fair. Do not pressure with fear and guilt.

There is no fear in love
Perfect love drives out all fear   **1 John 4:18**

DOUBLE STANDARD

"Do what I say, not what I do" has messed up many children in their quest to understand the difference between right and wrong. The hypocrisy of the double standard has its price: children who will some day judge you with disgust, or (far worse) will become the same type of person.

When a disgraced President told a nation—"nothing is illegal if it is done by the President" we shook our heads in disbelief and disgust. Yet many parents are convinced of this two-faced standard that demands respect for what is not expected.

Remember: It is not what you say or even what you do that is influencing your children. It is *who you are* that they seek for imitation. If something is good or okay for you, then it is okay for them. You do not have a leg to stand on if they copy your style.

Do not punish your children for vulgarity if your language is often punctuated with obscenities. Do not preach to your child about the value of religion, if you are too lazy to worship God. Do not, with a few exceptions, expect your child to do anything that you are not prepared to do yourself. Do not be hypocrites! You'll pay a high price later in life.

**What you are cries out so loud
I cannot hear what you are saying.**   **Indian Proverb**

BUILD UP!

Abraham Lincoln offers the suggestion to parents: "A person has the right to criticize who has the heart to help". Inconsiderate criticism is the noisy sound of hypocrites. If a parent is sincere, the patient and perhaps painful attention to correction will always accompany constructive criticism.

Many children simply compound their mistakes because the parent sacrifices very little time to teach otherwise. They saturate the child with biting sarcasm and create a self-hatred syndrome.

Negative criticism is always a defeating experience. Constructive criticism, likewise, is ineffective unless it is supported with a sincere and positive effort to help the child.

It is a sorry scene to see a young child who is disgusted with herself because she has been crushed with criticism and kept confused in her chance to change for the better.

If anyone has made somebody sad, you should forgive him and encourage him to keep him from becoming so sad as to give up completely. Let him know then that you really do love him.   2 Corinthians 2:5

BETTER THAN BEST ?

Perfectionist are never satisfied that their children have successfully accomplished anything—"Even your best isn't good enough". If the child comes home with four A's on the report card, the parents emphasize the one B.

Their own neurotic striving for the prestige of perfection keeps pushing their child. Eventually they produce a ten year old adult with a one track mind—I have to be better than my best.

Consequently, the child's relative failure makes her physically sick. She becomes neurotic about overcoming her weakness and cries herself asleep at ten years old—because she's a failure.

The parents have a nice trophy for their madness —a plastic little child who has one purpose in life—do or die.

Don't do anything from selfish ambition or from a cheap desire to boast. Be humble toward each other, never thinking that you are better than others. And look out for each other's interests, not just for your own.
Philippians 2:3

INVEST IN INTEGRITY

Parents who make a recreation of deals and deceit embroid a thread of dishonesty into the personality fibers of their children.

They do not break any laws. They simply tarnish them. The children learn the easy and lazy way of taking advantage of people. They become opportunists and trade trust and loyalty for profit.

It is really sad to see young children who live by the edict "Don't give a sucker an even break". They become sneaky and secretive and soon the parents find that their humorous episodes of deceit have educated a chronic little liar.

Invest in integrity. Honest people might not have all the luxuries of life but peace of mind and good children are the luxuries you cannot do without.

A scoundrel, he goes with a leer on his lips
Winking his eyes and beckoning with his finger
Deceit is in his heart, always scheming evil
He sows dissension
Disaster will overtake him and his fall will come.
                                        Proverb 6:12

SET THEM FREE !

Slavery has been supported by the axiom: "What they do not know will not hurt us." Some parents discourage higher education because "the children might get some wild ideas of not needing us."

They keep them dumb, dependent and depressed—needing the constant tender loving care of parents who keep them shackled to the house. They offer their children pity rather than personal pride.

Children are born to be set free and should be offered all the opportunities possible to acquire their own identity and strike out on their own.

The greatest culmination of a parent's pride is the day when the child can stand on its own and even leave "the nest" to fly its own way and soar to the heights of its dreams.

Nobody lights a lamp to put it under a bowl. Instead he puts it on the lampstand where it gives light for everyone in the house. In the same way your light must shine before people so that they will see the good things you do. **Matthew 5:15**

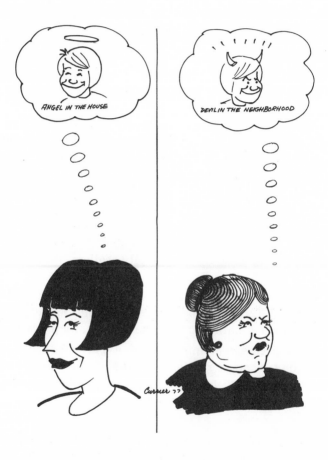

LOSING THEM ?

Parents who frequently tell their children to "get lost" wonder why they are so inconsiderate when they leave home to "find themselves".

They are shuffled off to someone else's care with the dictum—out of sight, out of trouble, out of aggravation for the parent. The parent insures the least amount of resistance by alienating the children to the neighbor's house or to grandma's kitchen.

Soon the child realizes that as long as he isn't a "pain in the butt" at home, he can do what he pleases elsewhere. He learns the schizophrenic game of acting out two personalities "home angel and street devil".

The teenage identity crisis is a traumatic experience for him as he tries to answer the question "Who Am I?". Often he goes off and tries to "find himself" by creating a new third identity.

Instruct a child in the way he should go and when he grows old he will not leave it. Proverbs 22:6

PLAYING FAVORITES

I suppose there are enough reasons to favor one child over another but parents should be ever cautious to suppress the natural inclination to have favorites.

Each child has a different purpose to fulfill and sensitive parental insight develops the best in each. Favoritism always neglects the potential of someone and the parent will pay someday with a jealous child.

Privileges should be measured equally and the same opportunities should be offered to all—even to the point of creating a family tradition. For example, if the oldest child gets an automobile for high school graduation then start saving for the others.

There will be times, of course, when one child will need more attention than the others but be careful to share affection, admiration and appreciation equally and justly.

Each one of us has been given a special gift.
Ephesians 4:7

TRUST

Trust is the inspiration for growth. When parents believe in children's goodness and potential they never pass a final judgement on them or retard them with a concluding prophecy. Their confidence is contagious as the child trusts his own abilities and achieves accordingly. As a child perspires a parent should be inspiring.

Goethe has a magnificent philosophy that many parents would do well to learn. He says: "If we take people as they are, we make them worse. If we treat them as if they were what they ought to be, we help them to become what they are capable to becoming."

A parent cannot say: "I know you like a book. You'll never change" because the best chapters have yet to be written. Nor can they write the book. They can only advise the direction of the script and not even then count on the conclusion. They can only hope that the teachings and trust they share will award their child with happiness and fulfillment.

Love has no limit to its trust
Love has no limit to its hope.   1 Corinthians 13:7

START EARLY

Someone should write a book entitled "What you should know about sex but you don't because your parents never taught you."

Sexuality's most important organ is the brain. So it is imperative that a child learn early and gradually the natural function and affectionate expression of sex. Of course the best sex-education is always taught in the context of love and commitment.

Every feeling should have its appropriate expression and parents can save the sexual desire from becoming a conquest, a curiosity or a crisis. They can teach their adolescents that a meaningful sexuality is not a "me" satisfaction.

Parents! You will be fighting against a culture that lends its support to sex as an appetite simply to be gratified, as a proving ground for an inferiority complex and as a service to be rendered for attention. You must start early.

Please do not neglect your responsibility and allow a school teacher, a social worker or a psychologist to explain what should be learnt at home.

Sexuality, like electricity, can run wild and out of control, or if properly channeled, it can light and warm our life.   Evelyn Duvall

COOL IT !

The fighting but forgiving parents are in love with one another but they are not creating a serene milieu for child development. If they do not get what they want, then they erupt like a volcano. The feeling is quite the same for people who live with it—fear.

Of course, they always kiss and make up but their passions are unpredictable, their tantrums are unbearable and the "peace" is unpleasant because it never seems to last long.

The children are on edge in expectation of the instant eruption with its hot lava of angry words and exploding fists.

All seemed to be peaceful and then suddenly it's "wartime" at the dinner table. Appetite and digestion are upset and a nice meal is spoiled again. The cursing finally turns to cooing and the white flag rallies everyone together for dessert but what a helluva way to live!

Healthy emotional growth demands a climate of consistent comfort. Parents! Please do something about your volcanic anger and allow your children to live in peace.

Where do all the fights come from?
They come from your passions
You want things but you cannot get them, so you quarrel. **James 4:1-2**

FACE REALITY !

Parents who take pills to pep up or slow down become a mixture of artificial moods and feelings. It is not surprising that their adolescent children see the Camelot escape of drugs when they have to confront the crisis of identity.

When parents are constantly taking pills they break down the credibility of their self-confidence and consistency which are very important for their child's imitation. Pills convey a false sense of sanity and security and offer a devastating surprise when they wear off. The person is still face to face with the mirror of reality.

Dis-ease is contagious and unfortunately children are inflicted with their parents' neurotic idiosyncrasies. Drugs are not the answer. They only make artificial parents who encourage children to seek safety under the same superficial shelter.

Get rid of your old self—the old self which was being destroyed. Your hearts and minds must be completely new. Acquire a fresh way of thinking.
Ephesians 4:22-23

SADISTS ?

Parents who aggravate their children with practical jokes and playful torture exhibit a touch of the sadistic. They enjoy hearing their children cry and then punish the child's traumatic fear with degrading remarks such as "You're such a sissy, can't you take it".

If parents were the butt of such jokes, I do not think they would fare as well. Yet they scold a child for being upset or afraid and make them feel inferior because they do not join in the sadistic laughter.

Laughter is the cruelest torture for a small child. There is no defense as the ridicule inflicts a wound that everyone seems to enjoy.

When everyone cannot join in the laughter
When someone sacred is made to appear funny
When someone's heart carries away an ache
It's a poor joke. **Anonymous**

COMPROMISE

Parents who bitterly fight over their religious convictions and struggle for their children's allegiance are making a mockery of their faith. The problem is not in the believing but in the pressuring of a child to choose one parent over another.

Please do not play tug of war with your children in the name of salvation. Offer them the opportunity to appreciate God without the confusion of bickering which claim a copyright on truth.

Parents! You should have come to grips with your religious differences before you were married. If you didn't, then at least try to discover the convictions that serve as a common denominator. Work for compromise.

If you do not use common sense, then the child will grow up with the distinct idea that God is the problem and retaliate by ignoring *any* religious or spiritual influence.

That would be a shame because I am convinced that a life without God is often a life without faith and hope. Please do not deny your children the enjoyment of a loving and merciful God who will offer meaning and purpose to their lives.

Do not fight over words. It does no good but only ruins the people who listen.　　　**2 Timothy 2:14**

STAY WITH THEM

Workalcoholic parents cannot understand why their children get so messed up. They sing the familiar refrain: "I've worked my butt off for these kids. I've given them everything. What else do they expect me to do."

Perhaps they expected their parents to help with the Cub Scout project, to ice skate in the park, or just to spend quiet evenings listening to their fantasies.

Children do not feel loved by how much money is spent but rather by how much life is spent. Tons of time and barrels of belonging are necessary to support a child's confidence.

Remember: Parents are the first and best of teachers and everyone knows a child never learns if the teacher is always out of the classroom.

Someone will say I am allowed to do anything. Yes but not everything is good for you. I could say I am allowed to do anything but I am not going to let anything make a slave of me. **1 Corinthians 6:12**

USING PEOPLE

Alvin Toffler in his book "Future Shock" has described us as a throw-away society in a rental revolution. We discard what is not useful and rent on a temporary basis as we wait for a better opportunity.

This socio-economic phenomenon has unfortunately weaved its way into our behavioral relationships with people. Many parents have become pragmatic opportunists who use people to their advantage and discard them when their usefulness is not profitable. The examples in the business field are numerous.

They disguise their selfishness with the realism: "You have to take care of   1." They teach their children a new golden rule: "Do unto others first what you think they might do to you."

What do children learn? They learn that nothing is sacred, no friendship deserves loyalty and that everything is good that gains something for themselves. No wonder we have an insane and sick society that pursues one quest—selfish satisfaction.

Your life must be controlled by love, just as Christ loved us and gave his life for us.   Ephesians 5:2

TENDER TOUCH

Parents, please keep "in touch" with your children. Kiss them good-bye, good night and any good time that it seems natural. The tender touch of affection is an important sign of belonging. It makes a person feel worthwhile and does wonders for communication.

Affection is also a beautiful language for forgiveness and makes it easy for parent and child to reconcile. The bonus of affection is its precious gift to the human personality of warmth and sensitivity.

It is awful to see cold, cunning and calculating adolescents who could care less about anyone. Often the parents have the same characteristics. They do not show affection to each other and have little inclination to affirm their children with an embrace.

Affection is such a human experience. Parents, please do not be self-conscious or embarrassed to hug and kiss your children. They need your warmth to grow as a tender flower needs the sun to grow.

Love one another warmly and be eager to show respect for one another. **Romans 12:10**

KEEP IT CLEAN !

Some children are assaulted each day with the crude vocabulary of obscene and vulgar parents. Sure they are loving people and good providers but they "gross out" their kids.

It is disgusting to hear the four letter slang of adults who think it is sophisticated to tell dirty jokes and talk about the sacredness of sexuality with sewerage adjectives.

Parents! Teach your little girl that she grows up to be a lady, not "a broad". Throw away your ex-rated magazines and pin-ups which somehow fill the void in your marriage and imagination and expose your children to healthy heroes. Teach the beauty of sexuality without the graffiti of the public bathroom.

Clean up your mind and give your children the chance to speak the English language and enjoy the normal development of their sexuality.

Your speech should always be pleasant and interesting and you should know how to give the right answer.
Colossians 4:6
It is not fitting for you to use obscene, foolish or dirty words.
Ephesians 5:4

COURAGE !

Some parents appear to be shy or bashful. Unfortunately, they are just weak. They are afraid of leadership. They lack courage and the backbone to make decisions.

What happens! Their adolescent children simply exist and learn to hide in the shadows. They recoil like a sissy snake when the schoolteacher expects achievement, when society demands availability and when the opposite sex calls for affection.

These children are usually pushed around and often insulted. The helpless fear that paralyzes their desire for assertion assures their eventual loneliness. They stir clear of any confrontation or possible criticism.

Quel dommage! The French say it well: What a pity! The spineless parent spinning out a copy of a coward.

Courage is the first of human qualities because it is the quality which guarantees all the others.
                                        Sir Winston Churchill

BE POSITIVE !

Misery loves company. Some parents relieve their own frustrations and failures by teaching their children how to be failures.

"If I cannot be a success how do you expect to make it" or "You have your mother's brains, you'll never get ahead" are a few of the one liners that kill initiative.

If life and luck have not offered you success, it does not have to be contagious. Do not let your cynicism kill "the chance of a lifetime" for your children. Encourage them to take advantage of opportunities and affirm them as they suffer disappointment.

If you are in a rut, please do not direct them off the highway and get them stuck in the mud so you can have company.

Sickness the spirit of a person can endure
But when the spirit is broken, who can bear this?
Proverbs 18:14

TAKE THEM SERIOUSLY

"Please take me seriously. I am not a joke" is a cry from adolescents suffering the sarcastic smirk of their parents who downgrade their dreams and laugh at their loves.

Their one-liners cut off communication and make the adolescent feel like a fool: "You're a dreamer." "How can you handle a boyfriend. You can't take care of yourself." "You don't know your own mind." "You must be kidding." "Don't bother me with your childish romances."

The adolescent finally decides: "Why put up with the aggravation" as she no longer shares her plans and problems, her dreams and desires. The parents soon lose their influence with their tin horn comments and the adolescent no longer appreciates their advice.

Parents! That is why you are the last to know. That is why they seek out the confidence and advice of their peers. That is why you have lost insight and influence.

If you are not sincere and serious with their questions, do not be surprised when they seek elsewhere for confidence and consolation.

Be sincere and serious in your teaching.   **Titus 2:8**

Currier 77

SPONGER ?

It is nice to see teenagers helping their parents by buying their own clothes, saving for college and paying for the odds and ends from their part time jobs.

It is kind of disgusting, however, to see parents "robbing" their children's birthday money and demanding a large share of their teenager's small paycheck. Teenagers still need a lot of financial help and they cannot be expected to do it alone even when they turn eighteen years old.

Parents! You did not create children to supplement your income. Do not pressure them with the pettiness of a paycheck. Teach them financial responsibility but do not expect them to provide for your extras.

They will feel used. Don't kid yourself—money is a source of separation and you risk the chance of your teenager despising you.

After all, children should not have to provide for their parents, but parents should provide for their children. I will be glad to spend all I have and myself as well in order to help you. 2 Corinthians 12:14

A BAD FEELING

Jealousy is a good word for a bad feeling. It makes a person feel jea-"lousy" and usually causes a cancerous deterioration of relationships and degradation of relatives.

Jealousy is the sickening infection of an inferiority complex. A person is so insecure that he/she is threatened by someone else's happiness. What an awful way to live especially for parents who claim to be satisfied and enjoy self-confidence. They are actually sneaky and spiteful people who inflict their children with the same dis-ease.

Parents! You can attain happiness without seizing another's. Teach your children to be happy when people are successful and enjoying good luck. Create peace and harmony in your own mind and in your home by appreciating what you have and not worrying what others have.

Don't brag about being wise and good if you are bitter, jealous and selfish. That is the worst sort of life. For wherever there is jealousy or selfish ambition, there will be disorder and every other kind of evil.
James 3:14-15

LISTEN!

Listening is a fine art for a person who is sincerely willing to help someone. Good parents listen twice as much as they speak. That is why God gave them two ears and only one mouth.

Parents, for all their intelligence and experience, are not always very polite. Sometimes they are downright ignorant. How many times have you heard your child's exciting story thru the newspaper as you grunt? How many times have you simply walked away and left your child speaking to herself?

How many times have you constantly interrupted her point of view and crushed her with yours? How many times have you smirked away his serious ideas with sarcastic laughter? How many times have you simply hollered: "Don't bother me"?

The child is left with the distinct feeling: Why say anything at all? No one wants to hear me anyway. Then parents wonder later on why their children are so distant and never share their deepest feelings with them.

Be steady in your convictions
Sincere in your speech
Be quick to listen
And deliberate in giving an answer.
                                    Ecclesiasticus 5:12-13

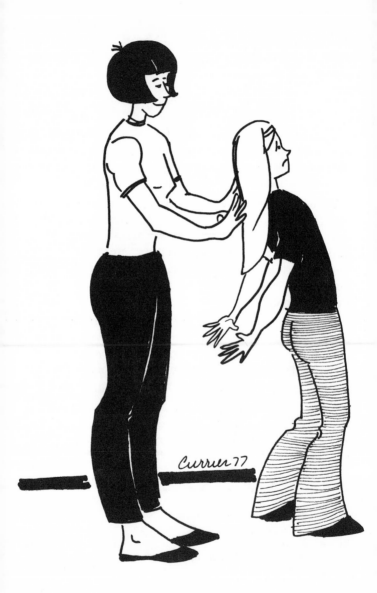

PEOPLE — PLEASERS

When someone says "I do not have an enemy in the world" he can be easily suspect of being a wishy-washy person—without backbone, strong convictions or definitive decisions.

Parents who try to please everyone and sacrifice their convictions in the process serve a poor example. There are far too many children with nervous stomachs and medicated with tranquillizers to relieve the tension: "I have to please everyone because I want everyone to like me."

Parents, please do not pressure your children to be popular with everyone. First, the price is too high. Second, it is impossible. Allow them the privilege of knowing people who do not like them. Maybe they are doing something right.

Each one should judge his own conduct for himself. If it is good, then he can be proud of what he himself has done, without having to compare. Galatians 6:4

PRIORITIES

Some parents neglect their work and family support to join clubs and crusades as a forum for their pride. It is fine to participate in clubs—as long as your family does not have to suffer for your involvement.

Actually, I find it quite revolting to see people praised for giving all their time to a club or a political party at the expense of their family. They are always available for strangers but their children never see them.

Parents! Your first priority is your family. Your second priority is your employment. After that, list your recreations as you wish.

You can gain a lot of respect, as St. Paul suggests, if you are a good husband, father and provider. The obituary notice will be long on success if you have proved yourself with those three titles —not how many clubs you joined.

Parents! I hope you do not experience the day when you realize your children are all grown up and you never took the time to really know them.

Make it your aim to live a quiet life, to mind your own business and earn your own living. In this way you'll earn respect. **1 Thessalonians 4:11-12**

LOYALTY

Children expect loyalty. Parents who impulsively understand "the other person" in the argument and disagree with the child will soon become the enemy as well.

Give the first moments of attention and understanding to your child's side of the story. If the child is wrong, never downgrade him in public. Simply say that the problem will be discussed later and in private.

There is no greater anguish than to be betrayed by someone you love. If the situation is serious enough, it will never be forgotten—and perhaps —never forgiven.

Of course, loyalty does not mean that parents sanction mistakes and misdeeds. Loyalty must always be explained in the context of integrity. Eventually, the child will expect loyalty only when he genuinely and sincerely believes he is right.

Let loyalty never leave you
Tie it around your neck
So that you will enjoy favor and good repute.
Proverbs 3:3

Currier 77

EGOMANIA

Parents who have illusions of their own grandeur inflate their ego by deflating their child's. Some are too afraid to be cocky with friends or strangers, so they dream their dreams and act out their superiority complex on their children.

The basic condescending concept: "I'm the expert and you are a dope" assault a child's confidence as it is translated into such degrading remarks as: "You little squirt, you'll never be as strong as your father", "You don't have the guts to be a man", "One thing I never gave you was my beautiful face and figure."

I'm amazed at how parents play their games to make themselves feel like "big shots" by shooting down their children and making them feel small and worthless. What does it accomplish? Nothing but the destruction of child's tender ego and the phony glorification of a parent's inferiority.

It is not right for you to be proud? Who made you superior to others? Didn't God give you everything you have? Well, then, how can you brag, as if what you have were not a gift? 1 Corinthians 4:7

Currier 78

GRANDPARENTS

How you care for your elderly parents is often how your children will care about you. May their blessing be yours and may your children treat you in the very same way you treat your parents.

The scandal of today's society is the treatment of elderly parents by selfish and insensitive adults who no longer include them in their life and treat them as a burden. Elderly parents are usually grandparents and your children will be enriched with their love and availability. Children need heroes, and grandparents can offer the simplicity and sensitivity that holds no disillusionment.

Likewise they can offer the storytelling, the respect for ethnic and cultural traditions, the common sense wisdom of experience and lots of time simply to do the things that parents have little time to offer.

Support your father and mother in their old age.
Do not grieve them
Even if their mind should fail
Do not despise them in your health and strength
For kindness to your father and mother should not be
forgotten.   **Ecclesiasticus 3:12**

Currier 77

SPARE THEM !

Parents who publicly embarrass and ridicule their children display their own disgusting deficiencies. It is awful to see parents make a scene at the beach, shopping mall or the neighborhood street as they execute punishment upon the little "criminal". Often they cause more of a disturbance than the child.

Usually, the child's mistake does not warrant the noisy parade of antics and adjectives that disturb polite people. The child feels like dying on the spot to escape the eyes of curious strangers. Parents, in the meantime, have made a fool of themselves and have taught the child that this is the way to relieve a problem—make a scene and embarrass the opposition.

A child can hope with private correction which does not damage its confidence or ability for self-assertion. Unlike public humiliation, the child can enjoy the comfort of knowing that no one knows. He has the chance to correct the mistake and still maintain his pride.

Always aim at those things that bring peace and that help strengthen one another.   Romans 14:19

Currier '77

INVEST IN THE FUTURE

Some parents are so intoxicated with their children that they absorb all their attention and association. They isolate a child from fantasy and friends.

Children should play with children and teenagers need other teenagers. Peer acceptance is very important and achieved only by trusting children to a privacy with friends which even excludes a parent's presence.

Allow your home to become a pleasant place for your children's friends. Let them play together and absorb the consequent noise and inconvenience in the interest of rearing normal children who learn early how to be a friend and how to get along with their peers.

When children become teenagers they normally seek the confidence and companionship of friends. If you have enjoyed the favor of their childhood friends they will want their teenager friends to like you as well. They will respect your opinion about the company they keep. So invest in the future and you will have the proper influence when it really counts.

**Your children are not your children
They came through you but not from you
And though they are with you
Yet they belong not to you.**   **Kahil Gibran**

Katie   Mike   Mom

"I DON'T KNOW ..."

Parents who have few hobbies are usually boring people and rear boring children. They do not instill the thrill to learn, to create and to fulfill the infinite possibilities of a personality.

They should excite their child to try something new each year and learn different skills: one year tennis, the next chess and perhaps another swimming. Help your children set a realistic, fun goal that can introduce them to the things people enjoy doing in this life.

It is sad for a young adult to say: "I do not know how to swim or play tennis. I hate to read. I don't know anything about cars. I don't know........
I can't........."

Not only do they miss out on loads of fun and lots of knowledge but they feel very inferior when they confront people who have been inspired to learn and enjoy hobbies.

Hobbies, likewise, offer the extra dividend of friends who are occupied with achievement rather than getting into trouble. Hobbies also unify families because so many of life's creative recreations are more fun when they are done together.

God has given each of you some special abilities. Be sure to use them to help each other, passing on to others God's many kinds of blessings.   1 Peter 4:10

CLEAN CRAZY

Some parents run their house like a "spit and polish" marine barrack. The child is always at attention for inspection.

They cannot play outside lest perhaps they get dirty. They can only play with one toy at a time less they clutter the house. They can only have one "visiting friend" and God forbid if they laugh or talk too loud.

These parents are usually inflicted with an even more agonizing neurosis—"the germ". They try to wrap the child in cellophane—free from contamination. I know one mother who actually refused her husband back into the house because he had cancer. This crazy woman thought it was contagious.

You can imagine the chance a child has to escape this inflicting neurosis which will be inbred and offer many unhappy experiences in the future.

Parents have the right to rest from their labors in the home that they have built but they should not let the home become their children's coffin. **Louis Evely**

Currier 77

ARE YOU A (——)?

There are affirming ways to correct a child but some parents use insane quips such as "Mommy is going to give you to the garbage man, if you don't shut up" "Do me a favor, go play in the traffic", or "You little (—) I'll break every bone in your body."

Correction is not suppose to threaten with fear but rather inspire to change. So the child is a nuisance today! Perhaps, it is social. He is lonely. Perhaps, it is emotional. He needs attention. Perhaps, it is intellectual. He does not realize the right way. Whatever the situation, parents can find just a little more patience to understand the problem and handle it with constructive, encouraging criticism.

Parents are suppose to be adults. If they cannot stay in control of the situation, perhaps *they* are the ("——") not the child.

Do not use harmful words in talking.
Use only helpful words, the kind that build up and provide what is needed. So that what you say will do good to those who hear you. **Ephesians 4:29**

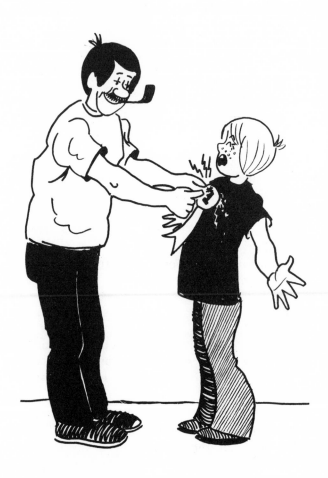

PARENTS' TROPHY

"You're nothing 'til you are   1" is the competitive ethic of some parents who take the joy out of achievement. They submit their child to a grueling confrontation to satisfy their own illusions of grandeur.

"Don't you want us to be proud of you?" or "You do not want to fail us, do you?" spur a child to stretch beyond the breaking point to please the petty pride of parents.

The child is not in control of his identity and destiny. He sits in the back seat of his own life as parents joy ride his talents to exhaustion.

The awards are affirming, the applause is pleasing but somehow he starts to feel like a bronzed trophy for his parent's cocktail table.

The same rules you use to judge others will be used by God to judge you.   **Mark 4:24**

PUBLIC PEACE

Parents who degrade each other with vulgar titles serve up a poor example to their children. They de-heroize each other and open themselves to the disrespect to divide and conquer.

Why respect "a moron", "an idiot", "a dumb ("—") or other unmentionable obscence monograms? Why listen to a parent who is always told "to shut up" and "mind your own business".

Spouses who mutually support and affirm each other offer a loving and consistent discipline that a child expects and respects.

If they do disagree, they should work toward unity in private and add some "class" to their parental image. Never, but *never*, should one spouse insult and degrade another in the public forum of their children's presence.

Make me completely happy by having the same thoughts, sharing the same love and being one in soul and mind.
Philippians 2:2

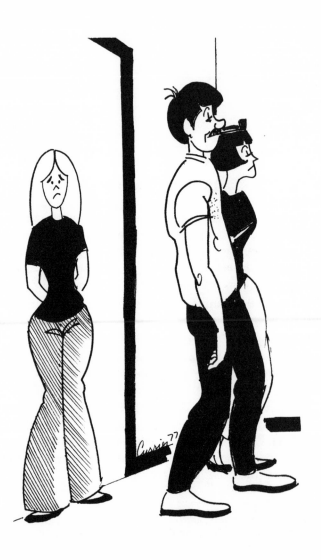

FORGIVE !

Silence and isolation are not constructive techniques for punishment. The solitary confinement ranges from the worst of totally ignoring a child to the best of cold, piercing glances with stinging monosyllables.

If parents can recall how they have been ignored, given the cold shoulder, or considered "a no—person". Then how could they possibly use this torture on a child? It alienates the child to an emotional leprosy with all its lonely consequences.

The musical refrain "Silence like a cancer grows" offers the best description of the deteriorating experience that results. The silent, indifferent treatment strikes at the vital center of self-confidence and paralyzes a child with the fear of being ignored.

Parents! You have the right to become angry but you also have the serious responsibility to be warm, tender and forgiving. No anger is righteous unless it is constructive and concluding with the embrace of forgiveness.

If you become angry, do not stay angry all day
Be kind and tender-hearted to one another
And forgive each other as soon as a quarrel begins.
Ephesians 4:26

SPEND IT !

The secret of making money is to know when you have enough so that it can be turned into experiences and offer the opportunity for creative leisure.

Parents work hard for money—not to hoard it but to use it as the medium of making a nice life for the family. Spend your money wisely but spend it! Enjoy life while you are healthy.

Cheap, miserable parents with a large savings account and impoverished children are weird people. They never go on vacation, the children are refused opportunities to develop their potential and learn one crazy lesson: save all the money you can for the future and never give any away. Get it?

To be poor is one kind of suffering. But a worst cruelty is have enough money and be cheap.

The love of money is a source of all kinds of evil. Some have so eager to have it that they have broken their hearts with many sorrows. 1 Timothy 6:10

TIME OFF

Pity the parent who feels so overworked that they forsake the child labor law. On Saturday morning everyone must be up early and ready to work all day around the house. Degraded is "the lazy child" who desires a extra few winks until 8 a.m.

They cannot play like children because they have to work like adults so that they can pay for room and board. Tough—for the parent who has to do a little extra work. It is all part of parenthood. Do not pity yourself if you have to pick up after your children.

Allow your child those enjoyable hours to have childish fun. Too few are the years that they can feel so free. Give them a few little chores to teach them responsibility but do not overburden.

Work hard and do not be lazy. Let your hope keep you joyful and be patient in your troubles.
Romans 12:11-12

NORMALITY

"Boys will be boys" and so will some little girls. Parents who overprotect their children are not doing them any favors. "You can't play baseball because you might knock out your teeth" is a typical version of many refusals that strike fear into little boys and create sissies.

Some children are so domesticated that they cannot even get dirty, let alone trespass beyond the boundaries of parental vision. They are wrapped in cellophane and become "nice, neat little sissy boys" the apple of mommy's eye.

When they grow up, they discover that a possible broken tooth does not hurt or embarrass them as much as the stinging criticism of their peers who have a repertoire of titles—the least being "he's out of it".

Parents! Do not stifle your child by always anticipating a disaster. Allow them to be normal children—excited about learning new games and interacting with their friends on the ballfield or even in the mud. A few broken bones are not as bad as a broken spirit.

God has given each of you some special abilities. Be sure to use them. **1 Peter 4:10**

REAL GIVING

"I've worked all my life for you and is this all I get—aggravation?" or "Spend your life for your kids and what do they give you? Suffering!" Some parents love because they want a reciprocal satisfaction. It is a selfish giving that says in effect: "I love you because by loving you, you will make me happy."

Of course, these parents will not admit it but their true feelings are uncovered when the adolescent ceases to please their every whim. They become vindictive and spiteful with the harsh demands: "If you can't live the way we live, then get out of this house." "If you get pregnant, you're no daughter of mine" "If you disgrace my name, I'll disown you".

The words "get" and "love" cannot even be used in the same sentence. They are contradictory terms that cannot live at peace with one another. The child who is exposed to their unnatural fusion will meet with the same disaster as their parents a feeling of being cheated because they didn't get back what they put in.

No greater love can one person have for another than to even give his life.   **John 15:13**

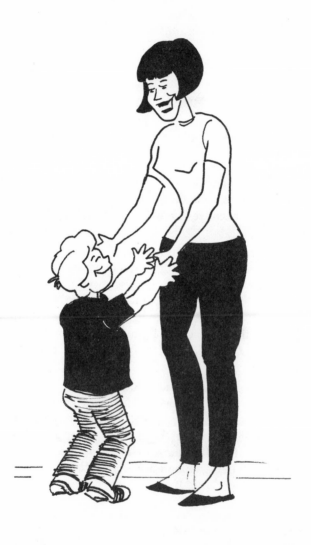

GENTLENESS

The parent who has to persuade with power and punches is a frightening example of a puny personality. The bully parent can instill fear for awhile but then the children grow up and they fear no longer. They simply hate.

The gentle parent—the gentleman and lady—can discipline for a lifetime with a tender love that breeds respect. No one likes a bully and if parents expect respect they must unfold the fist into a gentle hand again.

Various are the causes for parental violence: uncontrollable anger, inability to cope with a crisis, inferiority complex or simply the mistaken notion that "pounding out a kid" is the best way to teach him a lesson. Whatever the cause, the effect is always disgusting and parents should seek professional help to control their violent emotions. Remember: "Nothing is so strong as gentleness."

"Parents, do not treat your children in such a way as to make them angry. Instead, raise them with Christian discipline and instruction." **Ephesians 6:4**

EXPECT NOTHING

If we live long enough, we will hear ourselves say: "Sometimes the more we do for people, the less they appreciate it." Parents have already experienced the suffering of ingratitude but they must check their cynicism.

The proverb: "Better to have loved and suffered than never loved at all" should guide a new direction from disillusionment. If a child is taught to care-less, he will be cautious, cold and calculating. What an awful existence—lonely and afraid to get hurt. He will miss the best part of living—which is loving.

Parents, come to grips with the consequences of caring. Set yourself free from the petty little existence of "being hurt" and be a witness to the wonder and warmth of loving.

If you do good only to those who do good to you, why should you expect a blessing. If you give only to those from whom you hope to get back, why should you expect a blessing. No! Give and expect nothing back.
Luke 6:33-34

MEAN IT !

"A person is as good as his word" and if you cannot keep your word, do not make the promise in the first place.

"Promises, Promises! You never keep your promise" is often a refrain from a child's repertoire. They are promised the world "to shut up or simply to shape up." The child responds to the settlement, but is rejected in the satisfaction.

Better to be honest and straightforward than to be labeled as sneaky and a breaker of promises. Trust demands the consistent support of occasions when you are true to your word—even if it takes great personal sacrifice.

Learn the lesson early in your parenthood: children do not forget a promise as you think they will. When you offer false, unrealistic promises, you wash out your word and erode their respect. In other words, you lose ground.

When you make a promise, say "Yes" when you mean yes and "No" when you mean no.   James 5:12

Currier 77

FACING UP TO IT

Parents do a great disservice to their adolescent child by always getting him out of trouble. They pay someone off or use their influence to help someone forget. A far more loving yet painful experience is to teach your children the simple axiom: "Take the consequences of your actions."

Of course the parent who stands for integrity—despite the cost—should likewise stand by their children as they suffer the consequences. Their forgiving and affirming love will insure a fresh new start for him. They can help him look out the front windshield of his life with a new vision for the future instead of reminding him to keep an eye on the rear view of his past.

Happy are the parents who are not afraid of the mistakes their children will make because they have taught them the responsibility of taking the consequences and enlightened them to the capacity to change and start again.

You who live in a world of crooked people must shine among them like stars lighting up the sky, as you offer them the message of life. **Philippians 2:15**

BE REALISTIC

Self-righteous parents are an agony to live with. They mistake principles for pride and punish a child for daring to have an opposite opinion.

They "rule" their children and demand unreasonable restrictions to captivate their ideology. Varied are the forms of punishment for the child who steps out of line: lock-up from friends, limited activity under a watchful eye and the cold shoulder isolation for the hard core recalcitrant.

It is no wonder that the children become angry, frustrated and jump at the first chance of "escape": drugs, alcohol, runaway or early marriage.

The surest way to lose your children is to demand compliance with unrealistic rules and regulations that even you as an adult have not yet been able to observe.

Do you pass judgment on others?
You have no excuse at all, whoever you are
For when you judge others
But do the same things that they do
You condemn yourself.   **Romans 2:1**

FIRMNESS

A child needs discipline and correction if he is to learn responsible freedom. Some parents, however, in the interest of being "hip" and contemporary offer their child free license to come and go as they wish at an early age.

You are not doing them any favors by trying to be their "buddy" at the expense of Christian discipline. There is a time and place for everything. Someday they will be set free to meet their own challenges but children are still in training to acquire personal confidence. If you send them out too soon, society will make emotional hamburg out of them.

Do not be afraid to hold your ground on unpopular convictions but always persuade them with loving gentleness. Discipline can be firm and affirming without being unreasonable. Pray for prudence for yourself and patience for your children.

Better open reproof than voiceless love.

Proverbs 27:5

EXTRA PATIENCE

Children who have learning disabilities suffer the inferiority of not being as proficient as their peers. They cannot read or write because they do not receive the extra attention that parents must offer.

Do not abandon your slow child to the school system and then complain about the failure of the teacher. A slow child will catch up if parents care enough to consistently plug the gaps.

Once he loses sight of his passing peers he can easily give up and chose an anti-social life style that does not require the basic skills that he has failed to learn.

Be generous with the extra patience that a child needs to feel normal and confident that he can catch up. If the parent doesn't care the most then everyone else who tries to help will look like society's well paid professionals just doing a job.

The person who plants few seeds will have a small crop. The one who plants many seeds will have a large crop.   **2 Cor. 9:6**

LAUGH WITH THEM

Soap opera thrive on problems which prolong the plot for years. Some parents survive the same way. Everything is a major conflict and "life is the pits".

The children soon become the star characters in the series called "Born Losers". They never expect happiness in this life because there are too many overwhelming disappointments awaiting them. Just look at their parents. How could their life be any different?

The child is taught to be satisfied with self-pity, to enrich its conversation with complaints and to find something wrong with everything good that happens to them.

Parents! Life can be very simple. Please do not pursue problems. Leave them alone. Suffer when it is necessary but spend more of your energy enlightening children to the many beautiful experiences of being alive. Teach them how to laugh!

We are often troubled, but not crushed
Sometimes in doubt, but never despair
With many enemies, but never without a friend
Badly hurt at times, but not destroyed   2 Cor. 4:8-9

Curren 77

HONESTY

Parents teach their children to steal when they joke about the towels they took from the hotel, the cigarettes they lifted from pharmacy or the magazine they swiped from the news-stand.

They unwittingly encourage a child to try the same. But it is never "cute" to start a career of stealing that can turn to shoplifting and probably continue to more daring adventures.

Every human creature has tendency to larceny and a parent can cut down the odds by installing a healthy respect for honesty.

Of course, parents must come to grips with the consequences of their own honesty. Perhaps they will not enjoy some of the luxuries that others have gained. But freed from deceit they can convey the joy of detachment that is far more exciting than dishonesty.

You teach others—why don't you teach yourself? You preach "Do not steal" but do you steal yourself?
Romans 2:21

Currier 77

SPEAK WELL

"If you cannot say anything good about a person, do not say anything at all." Many parents do not accept the wisdom of this idiom. They educate their children to learn the language of gossip, the lingo of cynical satire and vulgar adjectives of petty jealousy.

They rear children who have little class and a lot less courtesy. The consequences are fracturing: few friends and many fights.

It is always fascinating to behold parents who are ladies and gentlemen. They are prudent and polite and so in control of themselves that they do not fall victim to the pettiness of "people picking". Their children grow up to be nice people.

Remember: Great people talk about ideas
Average people talk about events
Small people talk about people.

If you want a happy, good life then keep control of your tongue and guard your lips.   1 Peter 3:10

RE - CREATE

There is more to living than just working. There are ideas and experiences to pursue. There are people to meet and places to go. There are dreams of excellence and heights for the spirit to soar.

The work ethic is good but can offer a boring routine of: work, eat and sleep which "grounds the spirit" of a child and makes her a "dull gull".

Parents must save time and energy to perform the divine act of "re-creating" which will be very "recreating"—a lot of fun for the family.

There are some chances to be taken, new adventures to be tried and attachments to be given up. The child should enjoy the dreams of "Jonathan", and she needs parents who are always inspiring and uplifting—realistically encouraging the child to reach for the stars and pursue a life of excellence.

"How much more there is to living instead of our drab slogging back and forth to the fishing boats. There's a reason to life. We can lift ourselves out of ignorance. We can find ourselves as creatures of excellence, intelligence, and skill. We can be free."
Jonathan Livingston Seagull

Curran 77

FULL OR EMPTY ?

There are two types of couples at cocktail parties: parents who ring with the genuine melody of crystal and those who klunk like the shallowness of glass. The difference in resonance is gained from the interior depth and breadth of a personality.

It is quite entertaining to see foxy ladies dripping with jewelry as they share pseudo—intellectual nonsense with their husband who is climbing the social ladder of success. X-ray their shallow interior and it is scary to see how little they have to offer their children.

Social success is such a waste if achieved at the expense of neglecting the spiritual and emotional enrichment of your children. Parents! Who are you trying to impress? Who are you trying to influence? Who do you think God will hold you responsible for? Successful fathers and mothers are more impressive than successful social butterflies.

You should not use outward aids to make yourselves beautiful as in the way you fix your hair or in the jewelry you put on. Instead your beauty should consist of your true inner self. 1 Peter 3:3-4

SPARE THEM

I'm sure parents do not like to be reminded of their foolish antics at cocktail parties or their absolutely stupid response to a crisis situation. Yet some parents consistently recall their child's "childish mistakes" and embarrass them as adolescents.

They center stage their "clown" for the entertaining laughter of relatives and friends and torture a young girl for once being a child.

There are too many young people who want to forget their childhood and start a fresh new life as an adolescent. Parents wonder why they are disgusted with their clown suit as they break from the family and seek a new identity.

My single purpose in life is to forget what is behind me and do my best to reach for what is ahead.
Philippians 3:13

TEST

YOURSELF!

This book has been addressed to good parents who love their children and sacrifice generously for their welfare. The reflections are not an indictment but rather an opportunity to perfect your parenthood within its realistic limitations.

There are many other factors which contribute to emotional child abuse including peers, the media and the school. There is also the reality of the child's free will to get messed up despite the love and sacrifice of good parents.

The following survey offers the chance for parents and children to understand their interrelationship with each other.

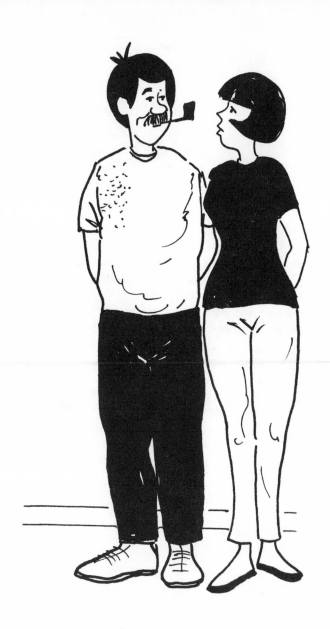

Have your parents stifled you with these one liners: NO   YES   OFTEN   SELDOM

1. I know you like a book. You'll never change.

2. If I'm not a success, how do you expect to be

3. You don't have any guts to get ahead

4. You can't do anything right. Let me do it.

5. You're not as smart as your older sister.

6. Don't expect miracles, you're not that pretty.

Have your parents stifled you with   NO   YES   OFTEN   SELDOM
these one liners:

7. Do you think you have the brains for college?

8. You'll be the death of me yet.

9. I've been around a lot longer, you'll do it my way.

10. If you get yourself pregnant, you're no daughter of mine.

11. Why don't you bring a little money into the house?

12. Don't bother me, can't you see I'm reading the paper?

13. You're a dreamer. Dream on.

14. You're a born loser. Can't you do anything right?

15. I'm ashamed of you. Can't you make me proud of you.

16. You were such an ugly baby.

17. Don't bring any of your friends around here.

18. Don't be such an idiot, you moron.

19. You're nothing 'til you are 1.

20. I've worked all my life for you and all I get is aggravation.

126

Do your parents often say:　　　NO　YES　OFTEN　SELDOM

21. I love you

22. I'm sorry, I jumped to con-
    clusions

23. I forgive you, let's forget about
    it

24. You can do anything you set
    your mind to

25. I trust you

26. I was wrong, you were right

27. Don't be afraid to talk to me

28. Honey, sweetheart ...

29. Don't be afraid, we'll stick by
    you

30. Try it, don't worry if it doesn't
    plan out

31. If first you don't succeed, try
    again

32. You are our daughter, we'll
    never be ashamed of you

33. We respect your opinions

34. We love all our children the
    very same

35. Take the consequences of your
    actions, right or wrong

36. Honesty is the best policy

37. You're beautiful

38. I'm proud of you

39. If you like it, try it

40. Hey, how about a kiss goodbye

Could you imagine your parents being able to write these books:

41. Do what I say, not what I do

42. What you should know about sex, but I didn't tell you

43. Even your best wasn't good enough for me

44. How my daughter caused my nervous breakdown

45. Vulgarity—How I taught my daughter how to curse

46. Stifling—How I overprotected and overpossessed my daughter

47. What my children don't know won't hurt me

48. My spouse—the dumbest I know

49. I only go to Church when there is a crisis

50. The best way to get attention: holler and curse

51. Don't take your kids seriously, they bluff a lot

52. If I get miserable, so should my kids

53. Don't let your kids forget their failures

54. My job first! My kids, when I get to them!

55. I don't get mushy with kisses and affection

Comment on these few quotes:

56. "A person has the right to criticize who has the heart to help." Is their criticism more often negative than constructive? Do they try to help you overcome your mistakes?

57. "A pat on the back is better than a kick in the fanny." Have your parents been too severe in their physical punishment?

58. "Silence like a cancer grows." Have your parents often used the silent treatment as a weapon against you?

59. "Don't give a sucker an even break." Do you think your parents have made you an opportunist—enjoying the wheel and deal—even if it is deceitful?

60. "Conversation is the heart of communication." If you were alone in the automobile with one of your parents for a long ride, would you feel comfortable—especially trying to keep a conversation going?

Please make any general comments about the influence of your parents if you feel an inferiority complex.

How do you feel about these questions:

61. Are you waiting to turn 18 years old so you can go off on your own?

62. Are you just tolerating your parents until you can get away to college?

63. Have you ever had thoughts of running away from home?

64. Have you actually run away from home?

65. Have you ever had thoughts of suicide because of aggravation at home?

66. Do you now trust and listen to your friends more than your parents?

67. Do you think your parents blatantly favor your brother or sister over you?

68. Do you think your parents have pressured you to be popular?

69. Do you feel your parents are jealous of you?

70. Do you feel your parents are very stingy with money?

71. Do you feel they are too preoccupied with trying to get money?

72. Do you feel your parents are overinvolved with clubs, church groups, or crusades?

73. If you became pregnant, would your parents suggest: "abortion"?

74. If you had a real problem, would you first tell your friend or your parents?

75. Do you live in a peaceful, loving home or is there a lot of fighting and bickering?

OTHER TORMEY BOOKS

now ...

TEENS ENCOUNTER CHRIST
The final edition of this indispensable Handbook contains timetables, photos, diagrams, lists, lecture-outlines, song suggestions and even a new Religion Program designed to capitalize in class on the dispositions created during the TEC weekend. Running now to over 300 pages, excellently printed and produced, it constitutes outstanding value at the following prices: single copy: $2.25; 10 copies: $20.00; 20 copies: $35.00. Postage extra unless prepaid.

TEENS
Encounter
CHRIST

The **TEENS ENCOUNTER CHRIST** retreat program aims at helping young people see the Christian message as a dynamic, personal invitation calling them to a deeper union with Christ in faith. It focuses especially on a weekend during which teens come together with a team of lay people (both peers and adults), religious and priests and, through prayer, discussion and reflection, learn what is the greatness of their Christian calling.

This is the Manual used for over 10 years at these weekends and here completely revised and updated by Fr. Andre' Cirino, O.F.M., Mrs. Francine Rogers and other collaborators. It not only offers a wealth of practical detail on every possible aspect of the TEC experience but includes for the first time similar guidance regarding REC (Residents Encounter Christ — the adaptation of TEC to correctional facilities) and HEC (Handicapped Encounter Christ). A completely new final chapter offers an attractive religion program designed to capitalize on the dispositions created during the TEC weekend.

ALBA BOOKS

CANFIELD, OHIO 44406
Phone: (216) 533-5503

An Interesting Thought

The publication you have just finished reading is part of the apostolic efforts of the Society of St. Paul of the American Province. A small, unique group of priests and brothers, the members of the Society of St. Paul propose to bring the message of Christ to men through the communications media while living the religious life.

If you know a young man who might be interested in learning more about our life and mission, ask him to contact the Vocation Office in care of the Society of St. Paul, Alba House Community, Canfield, Ohio 44406 (phone 216/533-5503). Full information will be sent without cost or obligation. You may be instrumental in helping a young man to find his vocation in life.